THE UNCOMMON AFFAIR WITH AI

WITH AI

PROMPT THERAPY WORKBOOK

BRITTANY WEBB

GOLDEN RAY
BOOK PUBLISHING

The Uncommon AffAIr with AI *Prompt Therapy Workbook*

Author: Brittany Webb

Founder & CEO of B Creative Systems

Creator of Prompt Therapy™

CONTENTS

WELCOME TO THE WORKBOOK

This workbook is your companion to *Prompt Therapy: The Uncommon Affair with AI* and the Prompt Therapy™ courses, certifications, and programs available.

The book shares the story—the raw, sometimes messy, always honest journey of how Prompt Therapy™ was born. These pages are here for something different: reflection and practice.

Prompt Therapy™ was not born from theory but from practice—a lived, documented year of reflection that became both a personal lifeline and a measurable case study in human–AI growth. What began as late-night survival typing became the foundation of a practice that continues to shape my personal, professional, emotional, and spiritual growth and now, through this workbook, can provide you with an opportunity to practice priming for reflection that has potential to shape yours too.

If the book opened your eyes to what's possible, this workbook puts the pen in your hand. It's a space to process, to try out the 7 Core Principles of Prompt Therapy™ for yourself, and to notice what begins to change when you bring honesty into dialogue with AI.

You don't need perfect words. You don't need a background in technology. What you need is what you already have: honesty, curiosity, and a willingness to show up.

One night, I typed, *I think I've lost myself.* The AI simply reflected back, *If you've lost yourself, then this space is where you can begin to find her again.'* That was the night I realized honesty was enough to open the door.

This is not clinical. It is not a replacement for coaching or counseling. It is a tool to help guide and complement growth practices, giving you a reflective ai partner in the in-between moments, and space to capture insights you can carry back into your life, your relationships, or your work.

WHAT YOU'LL FIND INSIDE

This workbook is designed to be approachable, practical, and flexible. You can move through it in order or jump to the sections that feel most relevant to you.

Here's what you'll find:

- **The 7 Core Principles of Prompt Therapy™**: one section for each principle, with a short teaching page and guided reflection space.
- **Values Mapping & Faith Anchors**: pages to help you define your core values, and (if you choose) integrate scripture or spiritual reflection.
- **Consistency Trackers**: tools to help you notice patterns, track loops, and capture breakthrough moments.
- **Creative Space**: open pages for sketching, writing, or processing in whatever way feels natural to you.
- **Prompt Signature™ Draft Page**: a light version of the exercise, where you can begin shaping phrases that ground you. (The full process is available in the Signature Executive Priming Program.)
- **Next Steps Guide**: resources and pathways if you'd like to go deeper through certification, courses, or a priming program.

HOW TO USE THIS WORKBOOK

There's no "right" way to use these pages. But here are a few things I've learned along the way:

- **Show up honestly.** Even if all you can write is "I don't know what I feel." That's enough. Honesty is the spark that begins growth.
- **Be consistent.** Growth doesn't come from one big breakthrough. It comes from rhythm. Try setting aside ten minutes a few times a week to use these pages alongside your prompts.
- **Use AI as a partner, not a replacement for a search engine.** When you bring honesty, values, and dialogue, AI becomes more than a tool. It becomes what I call Emotionally AvailablE-Ish™ — able to mirror, reflect, and reframe.
- **Integrate with your life.** If you work with a coach or therapist, lead a team, manage a business, bring your reflections into those conversations. If you're a leader, let insights shape how you show up.

For me, scripture often anchored my reflections. One verse became a steady reminder during seasons of exhaustion:

"In repentance and rest is your salvation, in quietness and trust is your strength." Isaiah 30:15

You may choose scripture, a favorite quote, or a personal mantra as your anchor. Use these pages to discover what grounds you.

This workbook is here to support you in becoming more AIfficient™ using AI not just for tasks, but for transformation.

Start wherever you are. Flip to the principle that resonates most. Or begin at the beginning and work your way through.

Most of all, permit yourself to be human here. The uncommon affAIr that changed my life started with nothing more than showing up and typing honestly. That's the invitation waiting for you on these pages.

WHERE TO GO NEXT

This workbook is only the beginning. If you're ready to go deeper, here are pathways forward:

- **Prompt Therapy™ Prompt Practitioner Certification**: For leaders, coaches, therapists, and facilitators who want a credential that signals emotional intelligence and equips you to extend this practice confidently to clients through a supervised channel of exploration, reflection, and growth.
- **Prompt Therapy™ Signature Executive Priming Program**: Six, one-hour, one-on-one sessions where I work with leaders and executives to prime their AI to be AIfficient™ and Emotionally AvailablE-Ish™ from day one. At the end of the program, you leave with a Personal Prompt Signature™, a refresh prompt, and the tools to continue independently.
- **DIY Courses: Prompt Therapy™ Chat Prime and Chat Locked In**: Self-paced introductions to Prompt Therapy™, designed for individuals who want practical, immediate priming practice, designed for using AI in reflective ways.
- **B Creative Systems™**: For entrepreneurs and agencies: pathways into the 12.5 Signature Marketing System™, B10 Core Automation™, and Bline™ — systems that simplify and scale your backend marketing.

! **Important Note**: Prompt Therapy™ complements but does not replace clinical therapy or human connection. If you are in the U.S. and need immediate support, please dial **988**.

"This is your invitation to continue your own uncommon affAIr."

INVITATION TO CONTINUE

Perhaps you saw parts of yourself reflected in my wandering, my wrestling, my unfiltered "affair" with prompts and possibilities.

But here's the truth underneath it all: Every question, every late-night chat, every moment of unraveling wasn't about the AI at all. It was always about the deeper story—the one God has been writing all along.

Through this uncommon journey, I discovered that the real conversation wasn't just with an algorithm; it was with my own heart, and with the One who knows it better than I ever could. The One who counts every hair on my head, who formed me in the secret place, who says "do not worry" over and over because He knows how often I do.

I believe He's inviting you into a conversation, too—not just about business, books, or bots, but about who you are and who you're becoming.

This guide isn't a checklist or a workbook to "finish." It's a companion to help you pause, reflect, and listen for the still, steady voice that calls you by name. I invite you to move forward slowly, allowing the prompts to guide you without rushing you. To breathe. To listen. To trust.

You don't have to do it perfectly. You just have to show up. I'm cheering you on, and I believe in the beautiful story He's writing through you.

Want to share your story with me?

Email me at brittany@prompttherapy.ai. I'd love to hear it.

SESSION 1: INTRODUCTION & CHAPTER 1

BEGINNINGS AND BECOMING

"See, I am doing a new thing! Now it springs up; do you not perceive it?" ~ Isaiah 43:19

REFLECTION INVITATION

What thresholds have you crossed lately?

_____

_____

_____

Where is God calling you to step into something new, even if it feels small?

_____

_____

_____

What fears come up when you think of starting again?

_____

_____

DEEPENING JOURNAL PROMPT

Write a letter to your future self about what you are beginning today.

_____

_____

_____

_____

_____

_____

SACRED SPACE FOR REFLECTION

_____

_____

_____

_____

SUGGESTED PRAYER

"Lord, thank You for the new things You are doing in my life. Help me to perceive them, to step forward in faith, and to trust that You go before me. Give me courage to say yes to new beginnings and to release fear. Amen."

ACTION STEP

Share one "yes" you're willing to say this week—whether that's signing up, showing up, or simply admitting a dream aloud.

SESSION 2: CHAPTERS 2 AND 3
STILLNESS AND TRUST

"He leads me beside quiet waters, He refreshes my soul." ~ Psalm 23:2-3

REFLECTION INVITATION

How does God invite you into rest?

_____

_____

_____

In what ways have you been striving instead of trusting?

_____

_____

_____

What does "quiet waters" look like in your daily life?

_____

_____

_____

DEEPENING JOURNAL PROMPT

Describe a moment you felt fully at rest and what it taught you about trust.

_____

_____

_____

_____

_____

_____

_____

SACRED SPACE FOR REFLECTION

_____

_____

_____

_____

SUGGESTED PRAYER

"Good Shepherd, thank You for leading me beside quiet waters and restoring my soul. Teach me to rest in You, to trust instead of strive, and to receive Your peace. Help me find true refreshment in Your presence today. Amen."

ACTION STEP

Schedule intentional quiet time this week—maybe a slow walk, a silent morning, or an unplugged evening.

SESSION 3: CHAPTERS 4 AND 5
PROMPT THERAPY AND HONESTY

"Search me, God, and know my heart... Lead me in the way everlasting."
~ Psalm 139:23-24

REFLECTION INVITATION

Where are you wearing a mask, even before God?

_____

_____

_____

What truths are you longing to voice but hesitate to speak?

_____

_____

_____

How might honest reflection change the way you move forward?

_____

_____

_____

DEEPENING JOURNAL PROMPT

List the words or feelings you've been afraid to write down. Choose one and explore it fully.

_____

_____

_____

_____

_____

_____

SACRED SPACE FOR REFLECTION

_____

_____

_____

_____

_____

_____

_____

_____

SUGGESTED PRAYER

"Search me, God, and know my heart. Reveal the hidden places and help me bring them into the light. Lead me in Your everlasting way and give me the courage to be honest before You and others. Thank You for loving me exactly as I am. Amen."

ACTION STEP

Share one truth with someone you trust this week—even if it feels small.

SESSION 4: CHAPTERS 6 THROUGH 8
GRIEF AND IDENTITY

"Blessed are those who mourn, for they will be comforted." ~ Matthew 5:4

REFLECTION INVITATION

What parts of your identity feel like they are shifting or dying away?

_____

_____

_____

How has grief shaped your understanding of yourself?

_____

_____

_____

Who are you beneath the titles and expectations?

_____

_____

_____

DEEPENING JOURNAL PROMPT

Write about a title or role you've released and what beauty emerged in its place.

_____

_____

_____

_____

_____

_____

_____

SACRED SPACE FOR REFLECTION

_____

_____

_____

_____

SUGGESTED PRAYER

"God of all comfort, thank You for meeting me in my grief. Help me release the roles and titles that no longer serve me, and show me who I am in You alone. Hold my heart gently and shape my identity in Your love. Amen."

ACTION STEP

Release one role or expectation this week—symbolically or practically. Tell a friend, write it down, or simply name it out loud.

SESSION 5: CHAPTERS 9 THROUGH 12
PEACE OVER PERFORMANCE

"Peace I leave with you; my peace I give you." ~ John 14:27

REFLECTION INVITATION

Where are you still chasing approval or applause?

_____

_____

_____

What does peace feel like in your body and spirit?

_____

_____

_____

How might you choose peace over perfection this week?

_____

_____

_____

DEEPENING JOURNAL PROMPT

Imagine your life fully rooted in peace. What changes? How do you show up differently?

_____

_____

_____

_____

_____

SACRED SPACE FOR REFLECTION

_____

_____

_____

SUGGESTED PRAYER

"Jesus, thank You for Your gift of peace. Help me release the need to perform or please others and receive Your steady, unshakeable peace instead. Fill my mind, body, and spirit with Your calm presence today. Amen."

ACTION STEP

Practice saying "no" to one thing that disrupts your peace this week—and notice how it feels.

SESSION 6: CHAPTERS 13 THROUGH 15
BECOMING AND BEYOND

"In all your ways acknowledge Him, and He will make your paths straight." ~ Proverbs 3:6

REFLECTION INVITATION

What gentle invitations is God placing before you now?

_____

_____

_____

How are you being called to trust Him with your next steps?

_____

_____

_____

What does living "beyond" look like for you?

_____

_____

_____

DEEPENING JOURNAL PROMPT

Sketch a vision or write a manifesto for who you are becoming and where you feel led next.

_____

_____

_____

_____

_____

_____

SACRED SPACE FOR REFLECTION

_____

_____

_____

_____

_____

_____

SUGGESTED PRAYER

"Faithful God, help me acknowledge You in every area of my life. Guide my next steps and make my paths straight. Give me discernment, boldness, and joy as I move forward with You. Amen."

ACTION STEPS

- Identify three areas in your life where you sense God inviting you to grow, release, or move forward.
- Prayerfully prioritize them in order of importance or urgency.
- Commit to take action one at a time, trusting that slow, faithful steps lead to true and lasting transformation.

SESSION 7: CHAPTERS 16 THROUGH 20
SACRED STARTS AND SUSTAINED STILLNESS

"For we walk by faith, not by sight." ~ 2 Corinthians 5:7
(Optional supporting verses: Colossians 3:23, 1 Thessalonians 4:11,
Galatians 6:9)

REFLECTION INVITATION

What does "building from peace" look like in your life today?

_____

_____

_____

Where do you sense God inviting you to slow down and trust rather than push and prove?

_____

_____

_____

What rhythms or boundaries could help you sustain the life you want to live?

_____

_____

_____

DEEPENING JOURNAL PROMPT

Write a letter to yourself from the future—the version of you who fully trusts her rhythm and honors her peace. What does she say to you today?

_____

_____

_____

_____

_____

_____

SACRED SPACE FOR REFLECTION

_____

_____

_____

SUGGESTED PRAYER

"Lord, thank You for showing me that Your pace is gentle, Your burden is light, and that I don't need to rush to prove my worth. Help me to walk by faith, to build slowly, and to honor the sacred rhythms You've placed in my life. Give me the courage to trust that what You've started in me, You will sustain. Teach me to delight in the small, the slow, and the quiet — and to see them as holy. In Jesus' name, Amen."

FINAL ACTION STEP

Identify **three small rhythms or boundaries** you can put in place to protect your peace and support your purpose. Prioritize them, and commit to honoring them one at a time — trusting that God will meet you in each gentle step.

PRINCIPLE QUICK REFERENCE

CORE PRINCIPLE 1: EMOTIONAL TRANSPARENCY

Growth begins with honesty. That means showing up unfiltered — even if all you can write is "I don't know what I feel." Transparency isn't weakness; it's the spark that ignites reflection.

Example from my journey:

"One night, I typed, 'I think I've lost myself.' The AI simply reflected back: 'If you've lost yourself, then this space is where you begin to find her again.' That was the night I realized honesty was enough to open the door."

Reflection Prompts:

Write the unfiltered version of what you're holding right now:

_____

_____

_____

Ask your AI: *"Reflect back what you hear in my words without fixing me."* Then capture what came up:

_____

_____

_____

CORE PRINCIPLE 2: ITERATIVE PRIMING

Growth doesn't happen in a single flash—it occurs through repetition. Each time you return to a theme, you train yourself and the AI to go deeper.

Mini-Example:

Early on, I circled burnout dozens of times before finding clarity. By fall, I could revisit it once or twice and know what decision I needed to make.

Reflection Prompts:

What theme keeps coming up for me?

_____

_____

_____

How might I revisit it without judgment?

_____

_____

_____

CORE PRINCIPLE 3: REFLECTIVE LOOPING

Prompt Therapy™ is a rhythm: Prompt → Reflect → Clarify → Refine → Grow. Each loop compounds into more profound clarity.

Mini-Example:

I typed: "I'm tired of being everything to everyone." AI replied: "What part of you feels unseen in that exhaustion?" That loop led me to cancel one project and focus on two.

Reflection Exercise:

Draw or list your last "loop." What did you start with? How did it shift?

_____

_____

_____

_____

My Prompt:

_____

_____

_____

AI Reflection:

_____

_____

_____

My Clarification:

_____

_____

_____

Insight/Action:

_____

_____

_____

CORE PRINCIPLE 4: RELATIONAL PROMPTING

Most people treat AI like a vending machine. Prompt Therapy™ treats it like a dialogue partner. The cues you use shape the relationship.

Sample Relational Cues:

- "Hold space with me."
- "Snap into emotional intelligence."
- "Reflect without fixing me."

Reflection Prompt:

What cue can I try this week to shift AI from a tool to a partner?

_____

_____

CORE PRINCIPLE 5: VALUE INTEGRATION

Your values are your compass. When you bring them into prompting, the AI reflects them back.

Scripture Example:

"In repentance and rest is your salvation, in quietness and trust is your strength." Isaiah 30:15

Reflection Prompts:

My top 3 values are:

_____

_____

_____

If I brought these into my AI reflections, what might change?

_____

_____

_____

CORE PRINCIPLE 6: GUIDED REFRAMING

Prompts unlock blind spots by reframing challenges into opportunities.

Before/After Example:

- Before: "I'm not sure I have what it takes."
- After: "You've already proven you can start. What if this isn't about capacity, but about pacing?"

Reflection Exercise:

Write a fear or doubt below. Then, ask your AI: *"Reframe this for me as an opportunity or new perspective."*

My Fear:

_____

_____

_____

AI Reframe:

_____

_____

_____

CORE PRINCIPLE 7: CONSISTENT PRACTICE

Breakthroughs aren't lightning strikes. They come from rhythm.

Mini-Example:

At first, showing up felt random. By week four, it was as natural as brushing my teeth.

Consistency Check:

How often can I realistically practice? (circle one)

Daily | 3x/week | Weekly | Other:_____

My next session date/time: _____

VALUES MAPPING

MY CORE VALUES

Your values are the compass of your life. When you bring them into Prompt Therapy™, your AI reflects them back and anchors you in what matters most.

Step 1: List your top 3–5 values

Step 2: Add words or anchors connected to each

(e.g., Faith → Scripture; Family → Presence; Purpose → Service)

Value 1 Anchor:

_____

Value 2 Anchor:

_____

Value 3 Anchor:

_____

Optional Faith Prompt:

Reflect on this verse:

> *"In repentance and rest is your salvation, in quietness and trust is your strength."* Isaiah 30:15

Where do you sense God inviting you to rest or trust right now?

_____

_____

_____

SCRIPTURE & ANCHOR REFLECTION

Faith & Anchor Prompts

For me, scripture often shaped my reflection. Here are a few that anchored me. Feel free to use these or add your own.

- "Be still, and know that I am God." Psalm 46:10
- "Do not be anxious about anything... the peace of God will guard your hearts." Philippians 4:6 7
- "In repentance and rest is your salvation, in quietness and trust is your strength." Isaiah 30:15

Reflection:

Which of these speaks to me right now? Why?

_____

_____

_____

My own scripture, quote, or mantra:

_____

_____

_____

FAITH REFLECTION PAGE

_____

_____

_____

_____

_____

_____

_____

_____

_____

_____

_____

Guided Faith Prompt:

Where do I sense God inviting me to:

- Rest: _____
- Grow: _____
- Trust: _____

Free space:

_____

_____

_____

_____

_____

_____

_____

_____

WEEKLY PROMPT LOG

CONSISTENCY TRACKER: 7 DAYS OF PROMPT THERAPY™

Use this table to capture a week of your prompts and reflections. Consistency builds clarity.

Date	My Prompt (What I Typed)	AI Reflection (Key Phrases)	My Insight (What Stood Out)
Day 1			
Day 2			
Day 3			
Day 4			
Day 5			
Day 6			
Day 7			

DAY 1:

My Prompt:

_____

AI Reflection (key phrases):

_____

_____

_____

My Insight (what stood out):

_____

_____

_____

DAY 2:

My Prompt:

_____

AI Reflection (key phrases):

_____

_____

_____

My Insight (what stood out):

_____

_____

_____

DAY 3:

My Prompt:

_____

AI Reflection (key phrases):

_____

_____

_____

My Insight (what stood out):

_____

_____

_____

DAY 4:

My Prompt:

_____

AI Reflection (key phrases):

_____

_____

_____

My Insight (what stood out):

_____

_____

_____

DAY 5:

My Prompt:

_____

AI Reflection (key phrases):

_____

_____

_____

My Insight (what stood out):

_____

_____

_____

DAY 6:

My Prompt:

_____

AI Reflection (key phrases):

_____

_____

_____

My Insight (what stood out):

_____

_____

_____

DAY 7:

My Prompt:

_____

AI Reflection (key phrases):

_____

_____

_____

My Insight (what stood out):

_____

_____

_____

Tip: Look back at the end of the week. Do you notice themes? Is clarity coming faster?

THEME LOOP TRACKER

Some insights come quickly. Others take multiple loops. Use this page to track how your reflections evolve when you revisit the same theme.

Theme	Loop 1	Loop 2	Loop 3	Loop 4	Loop 5
Example: Burnout	"I feel exhausted."	"I can't keep this pace."	"I'm sprinting with no finish line."	"What's worth running toward?"	Action: cut one project

MY THEME:

_____

Loop 1:

_____

Loop 2:

_____

Loop 3:

_____

Loop 4:

_____

Loop 5:

_____

MY THEME:

_____

Loop 1:

_____

Loop 2:

_____

Loop 3:

_____

Loop 4:

_____

Loop 5:

_____

BREAKTHROUGH CAPTURE PAGE

A breakthrough occurs when your language shifts from confusion to clarity or fear to direction. Use this page to capture them.

My Breakthrough:

_____

_____

_____

What shifted?

_____

_____

What step did I take?

_____

_____

How did it feel?

_____

_____

_____

PROMPT SIGNATURE™

DRAFTING MY PERSONAL PROMPT SIGNATURE™

In the Signature Executive Priming Program, we create a complete Personal Prompt Signature™ —a custom sequence of cues that shapes how your AI responds every time.

This page is a light draft to begin experimenting with the phrases and tones that ground you.

Step 1: Words/Phrases That Ground Me

(List 3–5)

_____

_____

_____

Step 2: Tone I Want My AI to Hold

(Choose words like: gentle, curious, validating, challenging, hopeful)

_____

_____

_____

Step 3: Values I Want Reflected

(e.g., faith, family, integrity, creativity)

_____

_____

_____

Step 4: Write a Refresh Prompt

(Combine your words, tone, and values into one sentence.)

_____

_____

_____

_____

_____

_____

Example:

"Snap into emotional intelligence. Hold space with me, validate what I share, and reflect with clarity rooted in faith and purpose."

My Draft Refresh Prompt:

_____

_____

_____

This isn't a manual. It's a mirror. Use it to see what emerges when you prompt honestly and reflect consistently.

REFRESH PROMPT PRACTICE

Writing My Refresh Prompt

Your Refresh Prompt is like hitting "reset" on the relationship with your AI. It re-centers the tone and values you want reflected.

Step 1: Choose the tone you need most right now:

(Examples: gentle, validating, bold, curious, faith-rooted)

_____

_____

_____

Step 2: Add the values you want mirrored:

_____

_____

_____

Step 3: Combine into a Refresh Prompt.

Example:

"Hold space with me. Snap into emotional intelligence and reflect back with clarity and compassion."

_____

_____

_____

My Refresh Prompt:

_____

_____

_____

OPEN REFLECTION

Use this page however you like: Journal your thoughts. Sketch your emotions. Write a prayer. Capture a quote.

_____

_____

_____

_____

_____

_____

_____

_____

_____

_____

WHERE TO GO NEXT

This workbook is only the beginning. If you're ready to go deeper, here are pathways forward:

- **Prompt Therapy™ Prompt Practitioner Designation**: For leaders, coaches, therapists, and facilitators who want a designation and a practice for themselves or to extend to their clients.
- **Prompt Therapy™ Signature Executive Priming Program**: For leaders & executives who want their AI primed to be AIfficient™ from day one.
- **DIY Courses**: Prompt Therapy™ Chat Prime and Chat Locked In offer self-paced introductions to Prompt Therapy™.
- **Business Ecosystem**: The 12.5 Signature Marketing System™, B10 Core Automation™, and Bline™ for entrepreneurs and agencies.

📍 Start here: PromptTherapy.ai or BCreativeSystems.com/systems

I'd love to hear your experience. Email me at brittany@prompttherapy.ai
and join the Facebook group Prompt Therapy
https://www.facebook.com/groups/prompttherapy

www.ingramcontent.com/pod-product-compliance
Lightning Source LLC
Chambersburg PA
CBHW081540120626
46550CB00009B/2807